z

2.

2

Plea
You
or b
1/c
523
JNF

DISCOVERING Space

COMETS AND ASTEROIDS

Ian Graham

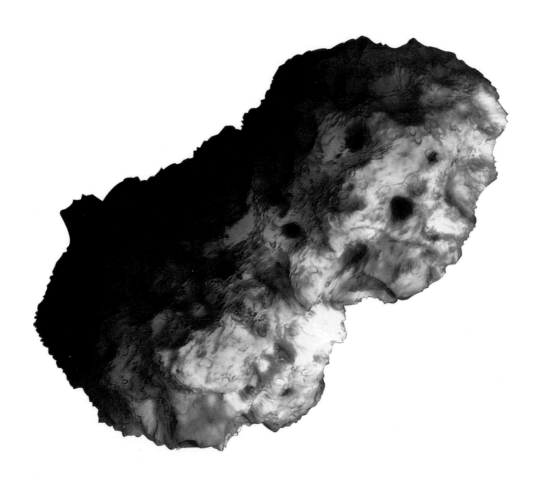

W
FRANKLIN WATTS

 An Appleseed Editions book

First published in 2007 by Franklin Watts

Franklin Watts
338 Euston Road, London NW1 3BH

Franklin Watts Australia
Level 17/207 Kent St, Sydney, NSW 2000

© 2007 Appleseed Editions

Appleseed Editions Ltd
Well House, Friars Hill, Guestling, East Sussex TN35 4ET

Created by Q2A Media
Series Editor: Honor Head
Designers: Diksha Khatri, Ashita Murgai
Picture Researchers: Lalit Dalal, Jyoti Sachdev

ISBN   978 0 7496 7573 8

Dewey classification: 523.6

All words in **bold** can be found in the glossary on page 30.

A CIP catalogue for this book is available from the British Library.

Picture credits
t: top, b: bottom, l: left, r: right, m: middle, c: centre
Cover images: Nasa: tl, Science Photo Library/ Photolibrary: tr, b,
Small images: Nasa/ JPL-Caltech: ml, Michael Puerzer/ Istockphoto: mr, Sebastian Kaulitzki/ Shutterstock: mc
Science Photo Library/ Photolibrary: 4b, 5t, 7t, 8b, 9b, 19t, 22-23 (background), 23t, 25t, 27t, William Attard McCarthy:
4-5 (background), Photo Researchers, Inc./ Photolibrary: 6b, 22b, The Bridgeman Art Library/ Photolibrary: 7b,
Roger Ressmeyer/ Corbis: 9t, Nasa/ JPL/ UMD: 10-11 (background), 20b, Nasa/ JPL-Caltech: 10b, 13t, 16b, 17t, Nasa/ JPL: 12b,
Nasa: 13b, 21t, 21b, ESA/ AOES Medialab: 15t, ESA: 14b, 15b, Nasa/ JPL-Caltech/R. Hurt (SSC): 16-17 (background),
NEAR Project: 18b, Oxford Scientific Films/ Photolibrary: 24b, 25b, Sebastian Kaulitzki/ Shutterstock: 26b,
Stephan Hoerold/ Istockphoto: 27b.

Printed in China

Franklin Watts is a division of Hachette Children's Books

Contents

Space rocks

As well as the planets, there are countless millions of smaller objects orbiting the Sun. These range in size from tiny specks of dust to huge rocks. There are giant snowballs in space, too.

Left-over chunks

The planets and moons formed from a giant cloud of gas, rock and ice swirling around the newly formed Sun, but not all the cloud was used up. Lots of chunks of rock and ice were left over and many of these bits are still flying around in space today.

Boulders of all shapes and sizes fly through the **Solar System**.

Spotlight on
space

Rocks flying through space are called meteoroids or asteroids. The only difference between them is their size. Meteoroids are space rocks up to a few metres across. Bigger rocks are called asteroids.

Comets are giant balls of ice and rock, like space snowballs.

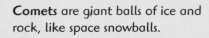

Most of the pieces of rock and ice that fly through space are far too small for us to see among the stars.

Crash or burn

Rocks from space often crash into planets and moons. The Earth's **atmosphere** protects us from most of them. The smallest rocks heat up as they plunge into the atmosphere and many of them burn up. When rocks hit a planet or moon without an atmosphere, they crash into the surface and make craters. The Earth's Moon is covered with these craters.

Comets – ice in space

Every few years, a strange fuzzy ball of light appears in the sky. It often has a long tail. In the ancient world, these unexpected visitors from space caused fear and panic. Today, we know what they are – they are called comets.

Space mountains

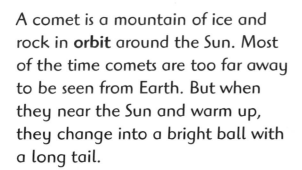

A comet is a mountain of ice and rock in **orbit** around the Sun. Most of the time comets are too far away to be seen from Earth. But when they near the Sun and warm up, they change into a bright ball with a long tail.

Comet facts

Comet		Appears every
Encke	▶	3 years 4 months
Tempel-Tuttle	▶	33 years
Halley's Comet	▶	76 years
Hale-Bopp	▶	2,400 years
Kohoutek	▶	75,000 years
Comet West	▶	500,000 years

A comet looks so bright because the dust it gives off reflects sunlight.

Growing tails

When a comet is warmed up by sunlight, some of its ice changes to gas. Gas and dust flying off the comet form a cloud around it called a coma. The gas and dust also stretch out into a tail. Sometimes there are two tails – a faint blue tail of gas and a brighter dust tail.

Gas and dust from a comet are swept back into a tail.

Spotlight on
space

Comets come from two streams of icy objects called the Kuiper belt and the Oort cloud. The Kuiper belt is at the outer edge of the Solar System. The Oort cloud is further away.

This 18th century picture shows how excited people were to see a comet.

Halley's Comet

The most famous comet is Halley's Comet. It appears in the sky every 76 years. At the time of its latest visit, in 1986, a fleet of spacecraft, including one called *Giotto*, was launched to meet it and study it at close quarters.

Regular visitor

Halley's Comet is named after the **astronomer** Edmond Halley. He saw it in 1682 and worked out that it was the same comet seen in 1531 and 1607. Records of Halley's Comet have now been found going back more than 2,000 years.

Giotto was one of five **space probes** sent to meet Halley's Comet.

Giotto mission		
Launched	▶	2 July 1985
Flew past Halley's Comet	▶	13 March 1986
Distance from Halley's Comet	▶	596 kilometres
End of mission	▶	23 July 1992

Giotto's photographs show jets of gas flying out of the sunlit side of Halley's Comet.

Giotto had to fly into the dust coming off Halley's Comet. The dust can cause a lot of damage so the front of the spacecraft was covered with a metal shield. It was hit by dust more than 12,000 times.

Dusty and crusty

Giotto's pictures of Halley's Comet show that it has a **nucleus** which is about 15 kilometres long and up to ten kilometres wide. The nucleus is made of ice mixed with dark, dusty material. The comet is covered by a thin crust of this dark material.

Halley's Comet is bright enough to see in the sky without a telescope.

Deep Impact

Scientists would like to cut up a comet so they can find out what it is like inside. They cannot do that, but the *Deep Impact* space mission did the next best thing – it dug a hole in a comet in space.

Collision course

The *Deep Impact* spacecraft carried a chunk of metal weighing 370 kilograms called an impactor. As *Deep Impact* flew towards a comet called Tempel 1, it let go of the impactor so that it would collide with the comet. The spacecraft's cameras and instruments then recorded what happened next.

Deep Impact mission

Launched	▶	12 January 2005
Impactor released	▶	3 July 2005
Impactor hit comet	▶	4 July 2005
End of mission	▶	August 2005

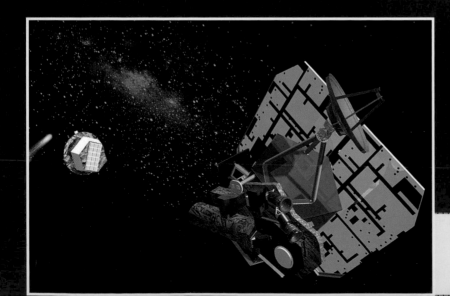

The impactor from *Deep Impact* flies towards comet Tempel 1.

Spotlight on
space

The comet Tempel 1 was discovered in 1867 by the German astronomer Wilhelm Tempel. The comet orbits the Sun every 5 years 6 months.

A flash of light

The impactor from *Deep Impact* hit the sunlit side of the comet Tempel 1. When it did there was a brilliant flash of light as sunlight bounced off the cloud of particles thrown out into space by the crash. The particles included dust and ice. The comet was held together by **gravity** only, so was easy to break.

The camera on *Deep Impact* watches as its impactor crashes into Temple 1.

Collecting stardust

In 1999 a space probe was sent to meet a comet in space, to collect dust particles from it and bring them back to Earth. No one had ever tried such a daring space mission to a comet before.

Wild-2

The comet chosen for this mission was Wild-2. It goes around the Sun every six years five months. The spacecraft, called *Stardust*, was aimed very carefully to meet Wild-2 as it sped through space.

Stardust mission

Launched	▶	7 February 1999
Flew past comet Wild-2	▶	2 January 2004
Returned to Earth	▶	15 January 2006
Total distance travelled	▶	3.2 billion kilometres

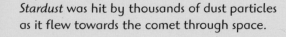

Stardust was hit by thousands of dust particles as it flew towards the comet through space.

Wild-2 was not discovered until 1978.

Stardust collected comet dust by catching it in a material called aerogel. Aerogel is a spongy jelly. When a dust particle flies into it, the particle slows down gently without being damaged.

Return to Earth

When *Stardust* had finished collecting dust from Wild-2, it headed back to Earth. As it passed Earth, it dropped a **capsule** containing the dust. Parachutes made sure the capsule landed safely. Space scientists are now studying the comet dust. Meanwhile, the *Stardust* spacecraft is still in space. It may be sent to visit another comet.

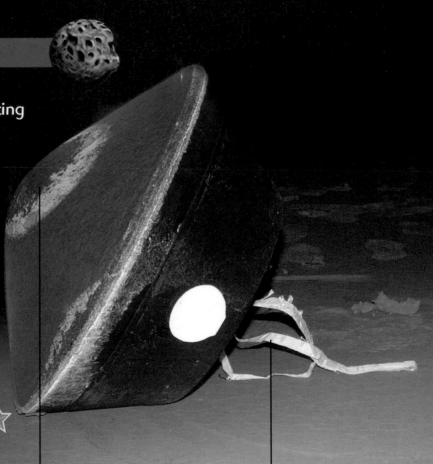

Stardust's capsule sits on the ground after returning from space.

Heat shield

Parachute straps

Landing on a comet

The *Rosetta* space mission will try to learn more about comets by landing a small probe on one. The spacecraft began its journey in 2004. It has such a long way to go that it will not reach the comet until 2014.

Orbit and land

When *Rosetta* reaches comet Churyumov–Gerasimenko, it will go into orbit around the comet. After making a map of its surface, a **lander** will be dropped on to it. The lander will be able to study the comet up close. It will send information to the **orbiter**, which will then send it to Earth.

Rosetta mission		
Launched	▶	2 March 2004
1st Earth fly-by	▶	March 2005
Mars fly-by	▶	February 2007
2nd Earth fly-by	▶	November 2007
Asteroid Steins fly-by	▶	September 2008
3rd Earth fly-by	▶	November 2009
Asteroid Lutetia fly-by	▶	July 2010
Arrival at comet	▶	May 2014
Landing on comet	▶	November 2014

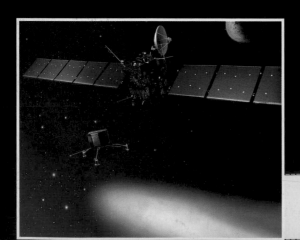

The lander from the *Rosetta* will chase comet Churyumov–Gerasimenko.

Rosetta was going to visit a comet called Wirtanen. But the rocket that was to launch it had an accident and so the launch was delayed. The mission was changed and Rosetta was sent to visit a different comet, one called Churyumov-Gerasimenko.

Rosetta swoops over the comet.

Rosetta's lander will fire a harpoon into the comet so that the lander does not float away into space.

Flight path

Rosetta is set to follow a very complicated flight path. It will fly past Earth three times and once past Mars. It will do this because the rocket that launched it was not powerful enough to send it straight to the comet. Instead, it will use gravity from Earth and Mars to boost its speed. Each time it passes Earth or Mars, the pull of the planet's gravity will make it go faster, building up the speed it needs to reach the comet.

Asteroids

Millions of lumps of rock orbit the Sun. They are called asteroids. Even though some of them are hundreds of kilometres across, they are so far away that they cannot be seen without a powerful telescope.

Where are they?

Most asteroids are in the space between the planets Mars and Jupiter. This is called the **asteroid belt**. There are asteroids in other places, too. Trojan asteroids are in the same orbit as Jupiter and there are asteroids that come close to Earth.

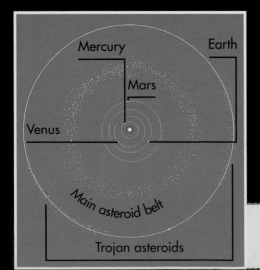

The biggest asteroids

Ceres was the biggest asteroid until 2006. Then astronomers decided that Ceres would be known as a dwarf planet.

Name		Size across the middle
Ceres	▶	940 kilometres
Vesta	▶	540 kilometres
Pallas	▶	525 kilometres
Hygeia	▶	430 kilometres
Interamnia	▶	325 kilometres
Davida	▶	325 kilometres

Space probes flying to the outer planets have to go through the asteroid belt.

Mathilde is an asteroid that measures about 59 kilometres across.

Spotlight on
space

Asteroids are not all the same. Some of them are very dark because they contain a lot of carbon. Some are made of light-coloured rock. Others are very shiny, because they are made of metal.

Changing direction

Asteroids sometimes change direction. They might be hit by another asteroid or they can be tugged by the gravity of a nearby planet. Sometimes when this happens, an asteroid is sent flying out of the asteroid belt and closer to the Sun. These asteroids are called **near-Earth asteroids**.

NEAR-Shoemaker

Asteroids are hard to study because they are so far away and difficult to see. Even through a powerful telescope, they look like tiny bright pinpoints moving among the stars. To see an asteroid up close, you have to send a space probe.

Visiting Eros

The *NEAR-Shoemaker* space probe was sent to study the asteroid, Eros. It spent a year orbiting Eros then, to end the mission, it slowly descended and landed on Eros. It is the first spacecraft to land on an asteroid.

NEAR-Shoemaker mission		
Launched	▶	17 February 1996
Flew past Mathilde	▶	27 June 1997
Flew past Earth	▶	23 January 1998
Flew past Eros	▶	23 December 1998
Went into orbit round Eros	▶	14 February 2000
Landed on Eros	▶	12 February 2001
End of mission	▶	28 February 2001

This asteroid is called Eros. It was the first near-Earth asteroid to be discovered.

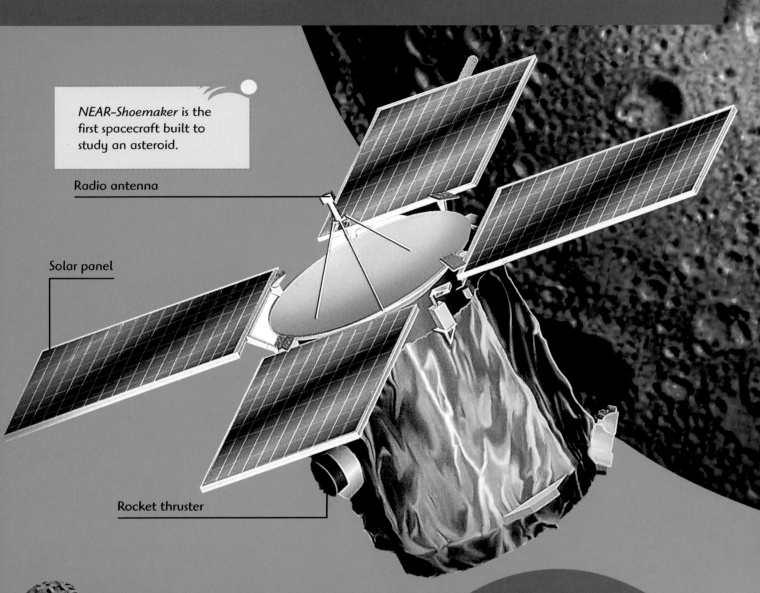

NEAR-Shoemaker is the first spacecraft built to study an asteroid.

Radio antenna

Solar panel

Rocket thruster

Surprise, surprise!

NEAR-Shoemaker's findings surprised scientists. They were amazed to see so much dust and so many rocks on the asteroid because they thought Eros's gravity was too weak to hold on to them. They found that most of the large rocks came from Eros itself. They were thrown out of a crater made when a meteoroid hit Eros a billion years ago.

Spotlight on
space

Eros is a near-Earth asteroid. It travels around the Sun every 643 days at a speed of about 87,000 kilometres per hour. That is more than 100 times faster than a jet airliner!

Space dust

Even the smallest bits of dust and grit flying about in space can be dangerous. These bits are called **micrometeoroids**. They can do a lot of damage, so the people who design spacecraft need to know about them.

Punching holes

Micrometeoroids are very small and they travel very fast. They are specks of rock and metal from asteroids and comets. Spacecraft have shields to stop micrometeoroids from punching holes in them. Some spacecraft have instruments that count the number of times micrometeoroids hit them, so scientists can learn more about them and how many of them there are flying around in space.

Micrometeoroid facts

Size	▶	smaller than a grain of sand
Weight	▶	less than 1 gram
Speed	▶	up to 80 kilometres per second

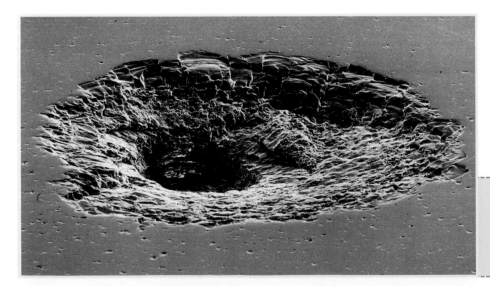

This highly magnified crater is actually a tiny pit in a space shuttle window caused by a micrometeoroid.

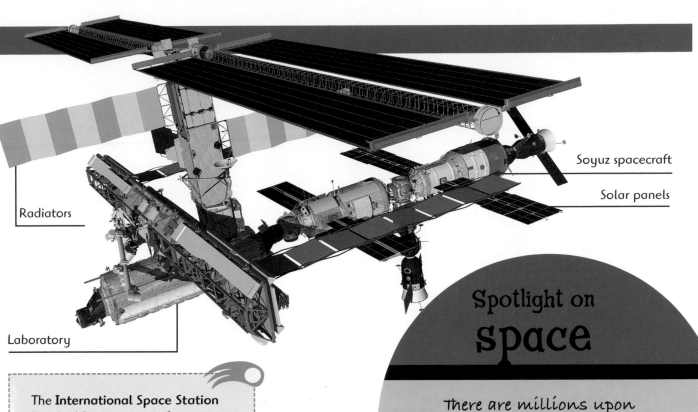

Radiators

Laboratory

Soyuz spacecraft

Solar panels

The **International Space Station** has shields to protect it from micrometeoroids.

There are millions upon millions of tiny bits of matter flying around in space. Not all of them are micrometeoroids. Some are flakes of metal and paint from old rockets and spacecraft.

Thousands of hits

In 1984, a spacecraft covered with pieces of different types of materials was placed in space. It was left there for nearly six years to see what would happen to it. The spacecraft was called the *LDEF* (the *Long Duration Exposure Facility*). When it was brought back to Earth in 1990, scientists found it had been hit 20,000 times.

The *LDEF* spacecraft showed how many times a spacecraft could be hit by space dust.

Shooting stars

On a clear night you might see a bright streak of light in the sky. It appears and disappears in a second. It is called a shooting star but it is not a star at all.

Hot rocks

When a meteoroid flies into the Earth's atmosphere, it heats up until it glows. The rock becomes so hot that it changes into gas, or **vaporizes**. It only takes a moment for a small piece of rock to vaporize completely.

Meteor showers

Shower name		When seen each year
Quadrantids	▶	3–4 January
Lyrids	▶	21–22 April
Perseids	▶	11–12 August
Orionids	▶	21–22 October
Taurids	▶	4–5 November
Leonids	▶	17–18 November
Geminids	▶	13–14 December

Meteors usually start glowing about 100 kilometres above the ground.

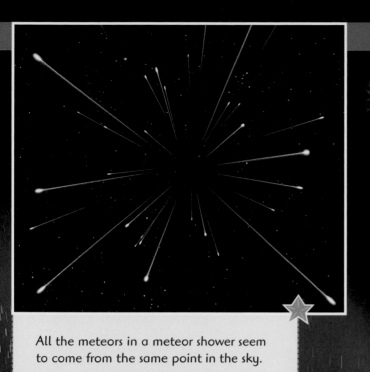

All the meteors in a meteor shower seem to come from the same point in the sky.

Left-over lights

You can see a meteor on any night, but there are lots more meteors at certain times of the year. These events are called meteor showers. They happen when the Earth flies through a trail of dust left behind by a comet. For example, the Perseids meteor shower in August is caused by a comet called Swift-Tuttle.

A heavy meteor shower can produce thousands of meteors an hour.

Spotlight on
space

Most meteors are produced by meteoroids about one centimetre across. Scientists have calculated that about 100 million of these plunge into the Earth's atmosphere every day.

Meteorites

Only the smallest space rocks burn up in the air. Bigger rocks fall all the way down to Earth. A space rock that lands on Earth is called a meteorite. Hundreds of thousands of **meteorites** fall to Earth every year.

Big rocks, small rocks

A meteorite can be as small as a full stop or as big as a house. Luckily for us, most meteorites are very small. The biggest meteorites hardly ever fall to Earth, perhaps only once in a million years.

The largest meteorite ever found is at Hoba West, Namibia in Africa. It is made of iron and nickel.

Amazing meteorites

Name		
Hoba West	▶	the biggest meteorite ever found, 60 tonnes
Williamette	▶	the biggest US meteorite, 14 tonnes
Orgueil	▶	contains carbon and diamond dust
Sayh al Uhaymir	▶	a meteorite from the Moon
ALH84001	▶	a meteorite from Mars
Heat Shield Rock	▶	a meteorite found on Mars by the rover vehicle, *Opportunity*

A meteorite heats up, glows and burns as it plunges into the Earth's atmosphere.

Rock history

Meteorites may have been flying through space for billions of years before they land on Earth. Scientists study them because they contain information about the history of the Solar System. Some meteorites come from the Moon or Mars. They were knocked off the surface and into space by rocks crashing into the Moon or Mars.

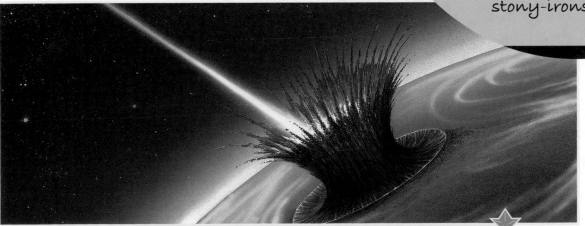

When the biggest meteorites hit Earth, they make huge craters in the ground.

Earth crashes

The Earth has been hit by asteroids and comets many times in the past and it may be hit again in future. Scientists are always scanning the sky, searching for any asteroids or comets that might be on a collision course with Earth.

Global disaster

If a giant comet or asteroid hit the Earth, it would affect the whole planet. Enormous waves would sweep around the world and so much soil and rock would be thrown up into the atmosphere that the Sun would be blotted out for months.

A massive asteroid crashing into Earth in the past may have looked like this.

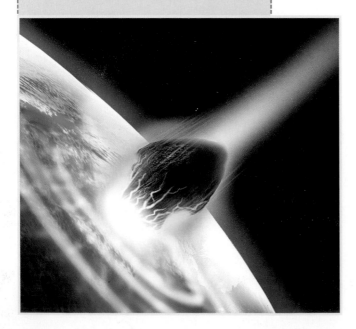

Earth impact facts

Object size		Impact on Earth
Up to 10 metres	▶	explodes harmlessly in the air
50 metres	▶	explodes in the air and causes damage on the ground
100 metres	▶	hits the ground and causes serious damage
1 kilometre	▶	massive destruction affects the whole Earth
10 kilometres	▶	few people survive anywhere on Earth

Whole forests in Siberia were flattened when a comet or asteroid exploded above the ground in 1908.

Several organizations watch the sky for any large objects that might be coming towards Earth. They include Spaceguard, NEAT (Near-Earth Asteroid Tracking) and LONEOS (the Lowell Observatory Near-Earth Object Search).

Saving Earth

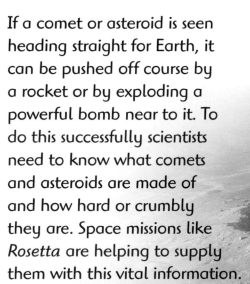

If a comet or asteroid is seen heading straight for Earth, it can be pushed off course by a rocket or by exploding a powerful bomb near to it. To do this successfully scientists need to know what comets and asteroids are made of and how hard or crumbly they are. Space missions like *Rosetta* are helping to supply them with this vital information.

This crater was made in Arizona, USA, 50,000 years ago when a meteorite weighing up to 300,000 tonnes hit the ground. It measures 1,200 metres across and 200 metres deep.

Timeline

240 BC
The first recorded appearance of the comet that is now known as Halley's Comet.

1682
English astronomer Edmond Halley sees the comet that is now known as Halley's Comet.

1798
Scientists measure the height of meteors above the ground for the first time.

1801
Italian astronomer Giuseppe Piazzi discovers the first asteroid, Ceres. In 2006, astronomers decide to make Ceres a dwarf planet.

1802
The second asteroid, Pallas, is discovered.

1803
Scientists work out what meteorites are.

1804
The third asteroid, Juno, is discovered.

1807
The fourth asteroid, Vesta, is discovered.

1826
Biela's Comet is discovered.

1845
The fifth asteroid, Astraea, is discovered.

1852
Biela's Comet appears in the sky but it is never seen again.

1858
Donati's Comet appears.

1866
Scientists work out that meteor showers are caused by comets.

1892
A comet is discovered for the first time by using photographs.

1898
The first asteroid to come closer to Earth is discovered. It is named Eros.

1908
A comet or asteroid fell in Siberia and caused widespread damage. It was named the The Tunguska Event.

1949
American astronomer Fred Whipple suggests that comets are like dirty snowballs – a mixture of ice, dust and bits of rock.

1950
Dutch astronomer Jan Oort suggests that comets come from a swarm of icy objects about one light year from the Sun. It becomes known as the Oort cloud.

1965
Comet Ikeya-Seki is bright enough to be seen in daylight.

1976
A bright comet, Comet West, appears in the sky.

1984
The *Long Duration Exposure Facility (LDEF)* is launched to study the damaging effects of micrometeoroids on spacecraft.

1985
The *Giotto* space probe is launched to photograph Halley's Comet.

1986
Giotto successfully takes close-up photographs of Halley's Comet.

1990
The *Long Duration Exposure Facility (LDEF)*, launched in 1984, is brought back to Earth by the space shuttle.

1992
The *Giotto* space probe flies past the comet Grigg-Skjellerup.

The comet Shoemaker-Levy 9 breaks into pieces as it passes the giant planet Jupiter.

1993
On its way to Jupiter the *Galileo* space probe photographs the asteroid Ida and discovers that it has its own moon, Dactyl.

1994
The pieces of the comet Shoemaker-Levy 9 crash into Jupiter.

1996
The *NEAR-Shoemaker* space probe is launched to visit an asteroid called Eros.

1997
NEAR-Shoemaker flies past an asteroid called Mathilde.

1999
The *Stardust* space probe is launched to visit the comet Wild-2.

2000
NEAR-Shoemaker goes into orbit around the asteroid Eros.

2001
NEAR-Shoemaker lands on the asteroid Eros.

2002
Stardust space probe flies past an asteroid called Annefrank.

2003
The *Rosetta* space probe is launched to visit the comet Churyumov-Gerasimenko.

2004
Stardust successfully collects particles from the comet Wild-2.

2006
Stardust returns to Earth with comet particles.

Astronomers name a new type of Solar System object called a dwarf planet. The largest asteroid (Ceres) and several other objects become dwarf planets.

Glossary

aerogel A spongy jelly used to catch dust particles in space.

asteroids Large pieces of rock, smaller than a dwarf planet, in orbit around the Sun.

asteroid belt The area between Mars and Jupiter where most asteroids are found.

astronomer A scientist who studies astronomy.

atmosphere The gas around a planet or moon. The Earth's atmosphere is made of air.

capsule A small spacecraft or a compartment inside a spacecraft.

carbon A chemical found in some asteroids and meteorites.

comets Balls of ice and dust in orbit around the Sun.

dwarf planet A large round object orbiting a star, but not big enough or special enough to be called a planet.

gravity An invisible force that pulls things towards each other. Earth's gravity pulls us down on to the ground. The Sun's gravity holds the planets, comets and asteroids in their orbits.

International Space Station A large manned spacecraft.

Kuiper belt Space beyond the planet Neptune where lots of

icy objects orbit the Sun. The dwarf planet Pluto may be a Kuiper belt object, not a real planet.

lander A spacecraft that lands on a planet, moon, comet or asteroid.

meteors Bright streaks of light in the sky caused by a meteoroid entering the Earth's atmosphere and burning up.

meteor showers Lots of meteors that seem to come from the same point in the sky, caused by the Earth flying through a trail of dust left behind by a comet.

meteorite A meteoroid that survives its journey through the Earth's atmosphere and hits the ground.

meteoroids Pieces of dust or rock in orbit around the Sun. Meteoroids bigger than about ten metres across are called asteroids.

micrometeoroids Tiny specks of rock or dust flying around in space.

near-Earth asteroids Big lumps of rock flying around the Solar System in an orbit that brings them close to the Earth.

nucleus The ball of ice and dust that forms a comet.

Oort cloud A swarm of icy objects that surround the Solar System far beyond the furthest planet. Comets are thought to come from the Oort cloud.

orbit To travel around the Sun, or a moon or planet.

orbiter A spacecraft that flies around, or orbits, a planet, moon, comet or asteroid.

Solar System The Sun, planets, moons and everything else that orbits the Sun, travelling through space together.

space probes Unmanned spacecraft sent away from Earth to explore part of the Solar System.

space station A manned spacecraft that stays in space for months or years and is visited by a series of crews.

vaporizes Destroys something by producing so much heat that it changes from solid or liquid into vapour (gas).

Index

WEBFINDER

http://www.esa.int/esaKIDSen/Cometsandmeteors.html

http://www.bbc.co.uk/science/space/solarsystem/asteroids/index.shtml

http://www.bbc.co.uk/science/space/solarsystem/comets/index.shtml

http://coolcosmos.ipac.caltech.edu/cosmic_kids/AskKids/asteroids.shtml

http://coolcosmos.ipac.caltech.edu/cosmic_kids/AskKids/comets.shtml

http://liftoff.msfc.nasa.gov/academy/space/solarsystem/meteors/meteors.html

http://www.nasm.si.edu/research/ceps/etp/asteroids

http://neat.jpl.nasa.gov/neofaq.html